MW01447425

FOR A FOOTBALL FAN WHO HAS EVERYTHING

A Funny NFL Football Book

Bruce Miller & Team Golfwell

For a Football Fan Who Has Everything, A Funny NFL Football Book, Copyright © 2022, Pacific Trust Holdings NZ Ltd. All rights reserved for the collective work only. No part of this book may be reproduced or transmitted in any form or by any means, electronic or mechanical, including photocopying, recording, or by any information storage and retrieval system, without written permission from the author, except for brief quotations as would be used in a review.

Stories and jokes in this book are fictitious and meant for entertainment purposes only. The NFL records in this book may have changed but are believed to be accurate at the time of writing.

This is the eleventh book in the series, "For People Who Have Everything." Cover by Queen Graphics. Images are from Shutterstock or Creative Commons.

ISBN 9798844637162 (Amazon hardcover)

ISBN 9798844636288 (Amazon paperback)

ISBN 9781991048110 (Ingram Spark Epub)

ISBN 9781991048127 (Ingram Spark hardback)

ISBN 9781991048134 (Ingram Spark paperback)

For a Football Fan Who Has Everything by Bruce Miller & Team Golfwell

The Jaguars haven't been to a Super Bowl. A group of businessmen is in Jacksonville for a company meeting. They decide it would be fun to catch a Jags' game. One of them calls up the ticket office to set it all up.

"Would we be able to get 50 tickets all grouped together?"

"One second, let me check.......... Sure, we can do that."

"Can we get them on the 50-yard line?"

"One second let me check...... Yeah, that can be done."

"Oh, by the way, what time is kickoff?"

"One second let me check........ What time can you be here?"

It's the same thing. "If you're mad at your kid, you can either raise him to be a nose tackle or send him out to go play on the freeway. It's about the same."

For a Football Fan Who Has Everything by Bruce Miller & Team Golfwell

-- **Bob Golic**, NFL defensive tackle from 1979-1992.

Two Detroit Lions fans died and went to hell. The Devil comes in on the first day to see the torment the men are going through. But to his surprise, the men are singing, and just having an enjoyable time. So, the Devil turns up the heat.

Again, to his surprise, the men are having fun.

So, on the third day, the Devil turns the weather into freezing. To the Devil's absolute shock, the men are jumping around, whooping and hollering.

When he asks why they are celebrating, one of them responds, "Cold day in hell, Lions must be in the Super Bowl!"

Food. "Football isn't football without food. How many layers of dip should I make? Not gonna lie, I'm here for the food. Tackling this game one snack at a time. I gotta prepare for those victory snacks. Pride, passion and pretzels I'm eating like a champion today."

-- Anon.

For a Football Fan Who Has Everything by Bruce Miller & Team Golfwell

Training. "What do you mean I snack too much while watching football? I'm actually in training to eat at Super Bowl party level."

-- Anon.

God loves the Jets. An Italian, an Englishman and a New Yorker are granted an audience with God. The Lord lets them ask a question about the future.

The Italian asks, "I'm a big F1 racing fan. When will Ferrari win another World Championship?"

"In 20 years," says God.

The Italian wails, "I'm an old man. I'll never get to see my team win a championship." He starts to cry.

The Englishman asks, "I'm a big soccer fan. When will England win another World Cup?"

"In 50 years," says God.

The Englishman wails, "I'm an old man. I'll never get to see my team win a championship." He starts to cry.

The New Yorker asks, "I'm a big NFL fan. When will my New York Jets win a Super Bowl?"

God starts to cry.

Let them tell you. "When you're good at something, you'll tell everyone. When you're great at something, they'll tell you."

-- **Walter Payton.** Former Chicago Bears running back.

Basketball vs. Football. "When I went to Catholic high school in Philadelphia, we just had one coach for football and basketball. He took all of us who turned out and had us run through a forest. The ones who ran into the trees were on the football team."

-- **George Raveling**, Former college basketball player and Coach at Washington State University, the University of Iowa, and the University of Southern California.

Sidenote. On August 28, 1963, Martin Luther King Jr. waved goodbye to an audience of over 250,000 people attending "March on Washington" and Raveling was there having volunteered to provide security on the podium with Dr. King. George asked him if he could have the speech. King gave him the original typewritten **"I Have a Dream"** pages.

George kept the original and was offered more than three million dollars for the speech in 2013 which he declined.

In 2021, George gave it to Villanova University. It is intended to be used in a long-term "on loan" arrangement.

No one noticed me. "Obviously, I didn't get looked at and didn't get recruited by Fresno State or any other school in the nation, to be honest. It has always been my goal to go into every game and show you why you should have recruited me, why you should have offered me."

-- **Josh Allen**. Some facts about Josh you might not know, Josh received no scholarship offers from any NCAA Division I program—whether in the top-level FBS or second-tier FCS.

San Diego State made him an offer to walk on, but Allen turned it down because Aztecs coach Rocky Long couldn't guarantee any playing time. In a 2017 story on Allen, ESPN journalist Mark Schlabach speculated on why Allen got so little interest out of high school, [1]

"At the time, Josh was about 6-foot-3 and 180 pounds. He hadn't attended the elite quarterback camps and wasn't a widely known prospect.

"His high school team didn't participate in many 7-on-7 camps because Josh and many of his teammates were busy playing baseball and other sports.

"He was the leading scorer on his basketball team and pitched on the baseball team, reaching 90 mph with his fastball." [2]

Despite that, in 2020, Josh led the Bills to their first division title and playoff victory since 1995.

He also set the Bills franchise records for single-season passing yards and touchdowns, while earning Pro Bowl and second-team All-Pro honors.

Josh brought the Bills to a consecutive division title the following year (the franchise's first since 1991) and became the first NFL quarterback to have a touchdown-scoring drive on every offensive possession of a game.

He is an avid listener of oldies music, which he says keeps him calm before games. His pregame playlist includes entries by Frank Sinatra ("That's Life"), Sammy Davis Jr., Elvis Presley, Paul Anka ("Put Your Head on My Shoulder"), and Billy Joel ("The Stranger"). [3]

For a Football Fan Who Has Everything by Bruce Miller & Team Golfwell

Josh Allen

Immediate concern. "What's weighing on my mind is how soon I can get a Bud Light in my mouth after this win."

— Peyton Manning.

Peyton's nickname, "The Sheriff" came from his tendency to call an audible prior to the snap.

Manning is thought by many to be one of the greatest quarterbacks of all time.

Peyton also said, "Pressure is something you feel when you don't know what the hell you are doing."

When asked who his toughest opponent was he said **Ray Lewis** Ravens linebacker was the toughest. Ray 6' 1" 240 lbs. led the Ravens' record-setting defense, which established a 16-game single-season record for the fewest points allowed (165) and the fewest rushing yards allowed (970), to victory in Super Bowl XXXV.

Lewis also became the second linebacker to win the Super Bowl Most Valuable Player Award, and the first to win the award on the winning Super Bowl team.

Shortly after beginning his NFL career, Manning started his own charity called the "Peyback Foundation."

The Peyback Foundation's mission is to help disadvantaged kids and focuses its efforts on Louisiana, Tennessee, Indiana, and Colorado.

Peyton is also third in career passing yards and passing touchdowns.

Finally, Manning is the first quarterback to have multiple Super Bowl starts with more than one franchise.

He was inducted to the College Football Hall of Fame in 2017 and the Pro Football Hall of Fame in 2021. [4]

Peyton Manning

I love my mother but... Years ago, Super Bowl XVIII featured the Los Angeles Raiders and Washington Redskins.

Before the game, **Joe Jacoby** a Washington lineman was quoted as saying something about how eager he was to win and jokingly blurted out something to the effect that he would run over his own mother if that meant they'd win the Super Bowl and claim the Vince Lombardi Trophy.

Matt Millen, a lineman for the Raiders was asked what he thought of Joe Jacoby's comment and responded, *"To win, I'd run over Joe's mom, too."*

For a Football Fan Who Has Everything by Bruce Miller & Team Golfwell

The Raiders won 38-9.

Astroturf vs. grass. "I don't know whether I prefer Astroturf to grass. I never smoked Astroturf."

-- **Joe Namath**. Some facts you might not know. Namath was the only athlete listed on the main list of Richard Nixon's political opponents which was made public in 1973 during the Watergate investigation, erroneously listed as playing for the New York Giants.

White House Counsel John Dean claimed not to know why Namath was included on the list and suggested that it may have been a mistake.

Joe Namath said he used to stay out drinking until 3:00 AM each night during the season.

In contrast, **Tom Brady** said when he takes a break, he has tomato slices on his gluten-free bagel according to jokes on Twitter.

On December 20, 2003, Joe had too much to drink on that day that was dedicated to the Jets' announcement of their All-Time team. During live ESPN coverage of the team's game, Namath was asked about then-Jets quarterback Chad Pennington and his thoughts on the difficulties of that year's team.

Namath expressed confidence in Pennington, but then stated to interviewer Suzy Kolber, "I want to kiss you. I couldn't care less about the team struggling." Joe later apologized and later entered an outpatient alcoholism treatment program.

In 2019, Namath said this incident was his main motivation to quit alcohol. He explained, "I had embarrassed my friends and family and could not escape that feeling. I haven't had a drink since." [5]

Broadway Joe also said, "When you win, nothing hurts." And in dealing with people, "I don't care what a man is if he treats me right. He can be a gambler, a hustler, someone everybody else thinks is obnoxious, I don't care so long as he's straight with me and our dealings are fair."

Having confidence is important to Joe. "I have to convince myself I know what I'm doing." And, when you know what you're doing, you can lead, "To be a leader, you have to make people want to follow you, and nobody wants to follow someone who doesn't know where he is going."

Finally on the bright side, Joe said, "When you have confidence, you can have a lot of fun. And when you have fun, you can do amazing things."

For a Football Fan Who Has Everything by Bruce Miller & Team Golfwell

Joe Namath

Has any game ever ended with a score of 2-0?

There have been 5 games that ended in 2-0 where only a safety was scored, and that score happened way back in 1938 when the Bears beat the Packers.

The strange thing is that there has been a total of 5 games that ended 2-0 but the Bears' win over the Packers in 1938 was the last one. No 2-0 games since then!

Easy game! "Football is easy if you're crazy as hell."

-- **Bo Jackson.** Former professional baseball and football player. He is the only professional athlete in history to be named an All-Star in both baseball and football.

Bo Jackson

You probably already know this. The NFL record for the most starts in a game during the regular season is 316 held by **Tom Brady** and the most starts in the playoffs is 46 also held by Tom.

Do you remember in 2021, Tom Brady became the first NFL quarterback to throw 600 career touchdowns? Also, in the fourth quarter of that game, Brady gave a Bucs' hat to a small boy in the stands who had a poster asking Tom to help him beat his brain cancer.

After the game, Brady said, *"That was really sweet, and he is a tough kid man. It puts a lot in perspective of what we are doing on the field. ... We all try to make a difference."*

You might not know

- Tom attended the University of Michigan and spent two years on the bench behind other quarterbacks.

- He was picked 199th in the NFL draft.

- Tom uses resistance training to help him stay flexible rather than traditional weight training as most athletes prefer.

- When he was a boy he played golf with his father.

- He usually goes to bed each evening at 9 pm and turns off all electronic devices at least a half hour before retiring.

- He rises at 6 am to get his usual 9 hours of sleep.

- His first job was a paperboy. His mother used the family van to help him with his route.

Tom Brady

Watching football games. "If a man watches three football games in a row, he should be declared legally dead."

-- Erma Bombeck.

In a recent study, "38% of Americans report watching two to five games per week…69% like to watch live sports more than just the highlights.

When it comes to sports highlights, the average American watches 1.3 hours per week, and the total average time spent watching any sports-related content per week comes to 4.17 hours." [6]

Longest postseason drought. The Arizona Cardinals, fka St Louis Cardinals, had the longest postseason victory drought in NFL history from 1947 to 1998.

That is 51 seasons without a postseason victory. The Cardinals started playing in 1898.

Not shy. "Marshawn Lynch wasn't shy. He believed you can't be charged for beating up on large groups of people-if you are carrying a football."

— **Matthew D. Heines**, Author.

Hits. "I like to believe that my best hits border on felonious assault."

-- **Jack Tatum**. Jack played safety from 1971 through 1980, with the Oakland Raiders and Houston Oilers.

He was popularly known as "the Assassin" because of his playing style.

However, according to his former head coach John Madden, Tatum was never called by that nickname during his playing career.

Tatum played his first professional game against the Baltimore Colts, in which he tackled and knocked out Colts tight ends John Mackey and Tom Mitchell. [7]

Dad Jokes. Q: Why didn't your neighbor's dog want to play football?

A: It was a boxer.

Q: What do you call an offensive tackle's son?

A. A chip off the old blocker.

Q: Which NFL team has the coolest helmets?

A. The one with the most fans!

Q: What do you get when you cross two football teams with the Invisible Man?

A: A game of football like you've never seen.

Q: Where do football players shop for a new uniform?

A: New Jersey.

Headlines: NFL Cuts One Team.

The NFL announced today that for financial reasons they had to eliminate one team from the league.

They've decided to combine the Green Bay Packers and the Tampa Bay Buccaneers and form one team, causing many layoffs but saving millions of dollars in costs.

They will be known as the TAMPACKS.

Unfortunately, they're only good for one period and have no second string.

Tom Brady's will to win. *"I'm a fairly good winner. I'm a terrible loser. And I rub it in rather good when I win."*

"I think my best asset as a player is that in the fourth quarter, with the game on the line, I have the desire to win and the feeling that our team is not going to lose."

"I didn't come this far to only come this far, so we've still got further to go."

"You wanna know which ring is my favorite? The next one."

-- Tom Brady

Longest winning streak in football. Between the years 1921-1923, a team named the Canton Bulldogs went 25 straight games without a defeat (22 wins, 3 ties) and won two NFL championships (1922,1923). This is still the record for the longest winning streak.

This is the reason the Pro Football Hall of Fame is in Canton, Ohio because of the Bulldogs' early success, along with the league being founded in the city.

Jim Thorpe, a Native American, Olympian, renowned all-around athlete, and was Canton's most-recognized player in the pre-NFL era. [8]

Jim was one of the most accomplished all-around athletes in history who in 1950 was selected by American sportswriters and broadcasters as the greatest American athlete and the greatest gridiron football player of the first half of the 20th century. [9]

Jim Thorpe began his career under coach **"Pop" Warner** and Jim played his best years in football and won two gold medals in track at the 1912 Olympics.

"Pop" Warner was one of the first to use the single wingback attack and invented the double wingback formation and is credited with developing the screen pass, reverse play, mousetrap, unbalanced line, rolling and clipping blocks, and others. [10]

Jim Thorpe

For a Football Fan Who Has Everything by Bruce Miller & Team Golfwell

No! Not Detroit! The Coach of the Detroit Lions had put together the perfect football team. But then his quarterback got blindsided and was out for the season with a knee injury.

Then his backup went down with a concussion. He tried the trading route, free agents, but nobody any good was available.

One evening while watching the news from Iraq, he saw a young Iraqi soldier with an amazing arm. The soldier rifled a grenade on a perfect arc into a 4th story window from 100 yards, bam!

He tossed another directly into a tight group of 12 enemy fighters 80 yards away, ka-bam! Then a Humvee passed, going 60 kph, boom! Another perfect shot!

The coach said to himself, "I got to have this guy. He's got the best arm I've ever seen!"

He tracks him down and convinces him to come to Detroit. The kid takes coaching perfectly, makes all the plays, and long story short, the Lions win the Super Bowl.

The Iraqi is now the Conquering Hero in pro football and a huge story. But when the broadcast team tries to interview him, all he wants is to phone his mom.

"Mother," he yells over the phone, "We just won the Super Bowl!"

"Don't talk to me," the woman says. "You abandoned us. You can't be my son."

The young Iraqi begs, "Mom, you don't understand! Our team won the biggest game here in the U.S. Thousands of fans are screaming for me. The U.S. President is going to call me!"

"I don't care," his mother snaps. "Right now, I can hear gunshots everywhere. Our block is like a ruin. Your brothers were beaten half to death last night, and your sister was nearly raped."

Then she says, "I can never forgive you for making us move to Detroit."

Amelioration. If Hannibal Lecter ran a 40-yard dash in 4.3 seconds, the NFL would just say he has an eating disorder.

    -- Anon.

Chasing. "It's a headache, chasing a guy around. I'd rather play against a quarterback that sits still."

    -- **Aaron Donald**, Defensive tackle for the Rams.

Aaron is 6' 1" 282 lbs. and is regarded as one of the greatest defensive players of all time. He commented on the new rule that came out that a player can't put his weight on the quarterback when taking them down. Aaron said,

For a Football Fan Who Has Everything by Bruce Miller & Team Golfwell

"It's tough. It's hard to really play defense now. I understand they're trying to protect players, but you tackle the quarterback, and they say you fall on top of them, you put your weight on them, and throw flags.

"It's tough on a pass rusher when they say you're taking the quarterback down and you fall on top of them and it's roughing the passer. There ain't much you can say, it's just tough.

I just don't get it, and if you let a great quarterback get time and comfortable, it's going to be a long day for us."

Aaron Donald

Baseball vs. Football. "Baseball players are smarter than football players. How often do you see a baseball team penalized for too many men on the field?"

-- **Jim Bouton**, Pitcher for the New York Yankees, Seattle Pilots, Houston Astros, and Atlanta Braves between 1962 and 1978

Undefeated teams in the regular season. The undefeated teams in the regular season were the 1934 Chicago Bears, the 1942 Chicago Bears, the 2007 New England Patriots, and the well-known 1972 Miami Dolphins. These are the only teams to go through a regular season undefeated. The **Miami Dolphins** had the only **"Perfect Season"** by being undefeated during the regular season and the postseason.

Two opinions from Ike.

- "An atheist is a man who watches a Notre Dame - Southern Methodist University game and doesn't care who wins."

- "The supreme quality for leadership is unquestionably integrity. Without it, no real success is possible, no matter whether it is on a section gang, a football field, in an army, or in an office."

— **Dwight D. Eisenhower** was the 34th President of the United States and a leader of the greatest generation During World War II.

General Dwight "Ike" Eisenhower served as Supreme Commander of the Allied Expeditionary Force in Europe and achieved the five-star rank of General of the Army.

He planned and supervised the invasion of North Africa in Operation Torch in 1942–1943 and the invasion of Normandy from the Western Front in 1944–1945. [11]

He played college football at Army as halfback for two seasons (1911-12) before breaking his leg in a game against Tufts College.

Presidents who played college were, Gerald Ford for Michigan, Ronald Reagan for Eureka College, Richard Nixon for Whittier College, John F. Kennedy for Harvard, and Donald Trump for New York Military Academy.

For a Football Fan Who Has Everything by Bruce Miller & Team Golfwell

Dwight D. Eisenhower

Of course! "The reason women don't play football is because 11 of them would never wear the same outfit in public."

    -- **Phyllis Diller**, Stand-up comedian, actor, author, musician, and visual artist, and best known for her eccentric stage persona, self-deprecating humor, wild hair and clothes, and an exaggerated - cackling laugh.

And have you ever wondered why doesn't the NFL like having women referees?

Because they bring up penalties from two years ago.

Get the guillotine. At the end of the 1976 Tampa Bay Buccaneers season with zero wins and fourteen losses, Coach **John McKay** was asked what he thought about his team's execution.

Without hesitation, he jokingly replied, "I'm in favor of it."

Four Football Fans. A Redskins fan, an Eagles fan, a Ravens fan, and a Steelers fan are climbing a mountain and arguing about who loves his team more.

The Redskins fan insists he is the most loyal. 'This is for the Redskins!' He yells and jumps off the side of the mountain.

Not to be outdone, the Eagles fan shouts, 'This is for the Eagles!' and throws himself off the mountain.

The Ravens fan is next to profess his love for his team. He yells, 'This is for everyone!' and pushes the Steelers fan off the mountain.

As you know the Ravens–Steelers rivalry is widely considered to be one of the greatest, most intense, and physical rivalries in the NFL.

Both teams are members of the American Football Conference North (AFC North) division. Since the Ravens' inception in 1996, they have played at least twice a year, often for divisional supremacy.

Both teams are known for fielding tough, hard-hitting defensive squads, giving their games that extra force of physical intensity. [12]

Qualifications for a lineman. "The qualifications for a lineman are to be big and dumb. To be a back, you only have to be dumb."

-- Knute Rockne

Knute Rockne was the head coach at Notre Dame for 13 seasons with over a hundred wins and 3 National Championships. He is considered by many to be one of the greatest coaches of all time.

Knute played football at Notre Dame and in November 1913, he was a member of the Notre Dame team that beat a much better Army team 35–13 in a game played at West Point.

Notre Dame's Charlie "Gus" Dorais, and Rockne, the Notre Dame came out with an offense with a powerful running game and long downfield forward passes from Dorais to Rockne.

The forward pass was being used now and then at that time and this game proved to be one of the first games where the forward pass was used the entire game.

Coach Rockne was considered one of the most motivational coaches in sports. Here is an excerpt from the Notre Dame Archives of one of his super speeches,

"All right, now. On the kickoff -- if we receive, the zone men will drop back to the receiver and block long -- that old Notre Dame style.

If we kickoff -- which the rest of the teams want -- let's run down fast -- just as fast as you can run.

"And then we go on defense. And on defense -- I want the center in and out of that line -- according to the situation. Use your old head!

"And I want you guards charging through as far as you can go -- on every play. Expect the play right over you every time --

"And the tackles -- I want you to go in a yard and a half -- and then check yourselves. Spread your feet -- squat down low -- and be ready with your hands and elbows, so you won't be sideswiped.

"But I want the ends in there fast every play. Every play, but under control.

"And you men in the backfield there, I want you to analyze it before you move. If they throw a forward pass, a zone pass, wait 'til you see the ball in the air -- and then go and get it!

And when we get it, boys, that's when we go on offense. And that's when we go to 'em

"We're going inside of 'em, we're going outside of 'em -- inside of 'em! outside of 'em! -- and when we get them on the run once, we're going to keep 'em on the run.

"And we're not going to pass unless their secondary comes up too close.

"But don't forget, men -- we're gonna get 'em on the run, we're gonna go, go, go, go! -- and we aren't going to stop until we go over that goal line!"

And don't forget, men -- today is the day we're gonna win. They can't lick us -- and that's how it goes... The first platoon men -- go in there and fight, fight, fight, fight, fight! What do you say, men! [13]

Knute Rockne

Say again? "I want to rush for 1,000 or 1,500 yards, whichever comes first,"

-- **George Rogers**, Heisman trophy winner and first round draft pick by New Orleans in 1980. Rogers was true to those confusing words and ran for 1674 yards in his rookie year.

Highest scoring game (so far). The highest-scoring game so far was in 1966 between the Washington Redskins and New York Giants, which produced a combined total of 113 points. The winning score was 72–41 in favor of Washington who led at halftime 35-14.

Hall of Famer, Sonny Jurgenson played quarterback for Washington and led the team to score a final total of ten touchdowns. Four of those were running, three passing, and one each on a punt, fumble, and interception return. They had nine extra points and a field goal. [14]

Trash talk joke. This is a joke to use to trash talk any NFL team, e.g., a Jaguar's fan. It goes like this,

A Jaguar's fan is at a bar with his dog watching the Jaguars play on TV.

When the Jaguars make a field goal, the dog struts down the bar and high-fives everyone he sees.

After another field goal, the dog high-fives everyone in the bar again.

The bartender asks the man what the dog would do if they scored a touchdown, and the man replies, "I don't know. I've only had him for three years."

Earned the right. "Anyone who's just driven 90 yards against huge men trying to kill them has earned the right to do Jazz hands."

— **Craig Ferguson**, Actor and comedian

Just joking! The Washington Redskins finally decided to drop their offensive name. The owner of the NFL Redskins, announced that the team is dropping "Washington" from the team's name, and it will henceforth be simply known as, "The Redskins."

It was reported that the owner found the word "Washington" imparts a negative image of poor leadership, mismanagement, corruption, cheating, lying, and graft, and is not a fitting role model for young fans of football.

The Winningest. "When I was a kid I was always the 199th pick that never had the body for it. People didn't think I'd play one year in the NFL, and now I'm going on my 17th year."

-- **Tom Brady**, the winningest quarterback in NFL history, Brady has won 243 regular season games and 35 postseason games for a combined 278 wins.

Brady holds a .769 winning percentage, which is the highest among NFL quarterbacks who have started 100 games. [15]

The mayor of the city of Tampa, **Jane Castor**, reported, "I told Tom, we are not discussing changing our city's name until he brings home that Lombardi Trophy. So, Tom and I will have that discussion in time. Yes, we will talk about that, changing 'Tampa,' since we are becoming a title town, to 'Tompa Bay.' We'll have those discussions."

Vision gets the dreams started. "Dreaming employs your God-given imagination to reinforce the vision. Both are part of something I believe is necessary to building the life of a champion, a winner, a person of high character who is consistently at the top of whatever game he or she is in."

-- **Emmitt Smith**, NFL all-time leading rusher (18,365 yards). [16]

Did you know? When Roger Staubach (Heisman winner) was playing for Navy, he used to play catch with his coach's son. Who was the coach's son? It was Bill Belichick.

Losing streaks.

The Chicago Cardinals team has the longest regular season losing streak, losing 29 consecutive games from 1942 through 1945. [17]

The 1976-1977 Tampa Bay Buccaneers hold the record for the longest losing streak (26 games) in NFL history.

That is a just bit surprising since Tampa Bay has a stadium that is a bit intimidating to opponents. This is because the crowd on the left side of the field goes shouts "TAMPA!" in a deep slow growling sound. Then the fans on the right side of the field immediately follow with a deep and long "BAY...!" That's repeated several times and is deafening and discouraging.

If you look at long losing streaks for away games, the 2007-2010 Detroit Lions hold that record at 26 games as well.

What about losing streaks at home? The 1988-90 Dallas Cowboys lost 14 straight home games. [18]

Who's the leader of the band that's made for you and me." I'm 6-foot-7, a big Black guy running down the middle of the field. ... I wear white gloves so quarterback Jay Cutler can see the white gloves when I wave them like Mickey Mouse."

— **Martellus Bennett,** Tight end

Why I like football. "Family members get to see you play. Ex-girlfriends that wished they wouldn't have dumped you -- they're questioning themselves right now. So, it's fun."

— **Steve Smith, Sr**. Wide receiver for sixteen seasons in the National Football League.

I'm too sexy. In 1998 People Magazine did its "Sexiest Men" issue and named **Rich Gannon** the "Sexiest Athlete" and dispatched a photographer to Kansas City to take publicity photos and told the photographer that the guy to take photos of was Kansas City's QB.

The problem was that the photographer had no idea what Rich Gannon looked like, so he took photos of the other Kansas City QB, **Elvis Grbac**.

Most say Grbac was not as good-looking as Rich Gannon. In the past People Magazine named athletes like David Beckham and former Miami Hurricanes football player and wrestler-turned-entertainer Dwayne "The Rock" Johnson each of whom earned "Sexiest Athlete."

When the magazine realized their mistake they didn't have the heart to tell Grbac, so they left it.

Grbac enjoyed being named the Sexiest Athlete of 1998 accordingly and the magazine described him as, "Leaping tall buildings in a single bound might be stretching it. But if you need a missile aimed with laser-like precision by a stalwartly handsome guy with a crew cut and a chiseled jaw, Kansas City Chiefs quarterback Elvis Grbac is your man."

The magazine ended the article with a quote from Elvis' wife, Lori, who said, "His personality makes him sexy."

Joshy Boucher? "My mom used to call me Joshy Boucher. I watched 'The Waterboy' so much, my mom started calling me Joshy Boucher." (True story).

-- **Josh Allen**

Overcome. "Being able to overcome obstacles and to demand the most out of yourself is a quality that everyone needs to be successful."

-- **Davante Adams,** wide receiver for the Las Vegas Raiders.

Davante grew up in California and attended Palo Alto High School where he led the school to a CIF state championship and played as a two-way starter.

He had 64 receptions for 1,094 yards and 12 touchdowns, and as a cornerback on defense, he totaled 44 tackles, including two for a loss, two forced fumbles, an interception, and four passes defended. He also played basketball and was considered a two-star recruit in that sport. [19]

Dear Diary,

For my fortieth birthday this year, my wife (the dear) purchased a week of personal training at the local health club for me.

Although I am still in great shape since playing football for 24 yrs. ago, I decided it would be a promising idea to go ahead and give it a try.

Called the club and made my reservation with a personal trainer named Vanessa, who identified herself as a 26-year-old aerobics instructor and model for athletic clothing and swimwear.

My wife seemed pleased with my enthusiasm to get started! The club encouraged me to keep a diary to chart my progress.

MONDAY: Started my day at 6:00 am. Tough to get out of bed, but it was well worth it when I arrived at the health club to find Vanessa waiting for me.

She was something of a Greek goddess with blonde hair, dancing eyes and a dazzling white smile. Woo Hoo!

Vanessa gave me a tour and showed me the machines. She took my pulse after 5 minutes on the treadmill.

She was alarmed that my pulse was so fast, but I attributed it to standing next to her in her Lycra aerobics outfit. Very inspiring!

Vanessa was encouraging as I did my sit-ups, although my gut was already aching from holding it in the whole time she was around. I enjoyed watching the skillful way in which she conducted her aerobics class after my workout today.

This is going to be a wonderful week!!

TUESDAY: I drank a whole pot of coffee, but I finally made it out of the door.

Vanessa made me lie on my back and push a heavy iron bar into the air, and then she put weights on it!

My legs were a little wobbly on the treadmill, but I made the full mile.

Vanessa's rewarding smile made it all worthwhile. I feel GREAT!! It's a whole new life for me.

WEDNESDAY: The only way that I can brush my teeth is by laying on the toothbrush on the counter and moving my mouth back and forth over it.

I probably have a hernia. Driving was OK if I didn't try to steer or stop.

Vanessa was impatient with me, insisting that my screams bothered other club members. Her voice is a little too perky for early in the morning and when she scolds, she gets this very nasal and annoying whine.

My chest hurts when I got on the treadmill, so Vanessa put me on the stair monster. Why the hell would anyone invent a machine to simulate an activity rendered obsolete by elevators? Vanessa told me it would help me get in shape and enjoy life. She said some other sh#t too.

THURSDAY: Vanessa was waiting for me with her vampire-like teeth exposed as her thin, cruel lips were pulled back in a full snarl.

I couldn't help being half an hour late; it took me that long to tie my shoes.

Vanessa took me to work out with dumbbells. When she was not looking, I ran and hid in the men's room.

She sent Lars to find me, then, as punishment, put me on the rowing machine.

FRIDAY: I hate that bitch Vanessa more than any human being has ever hated any other human being in the history of the world. Stupid, skinny, anemic little cheerleader.

If there were a part of my body I could move without unbearable pain, I would beat her with it.

Vanessa wanted me to work on my triceps - I don't have any triceps! And if you don't want dents in the floor, don't hand me the Barbells or anything that weighs more than a sandwich.

The treadmill flung me off and I landed on a health and nutrition teacher.

Why couldn't it have been someone softer, like the drama coach or the choir director?

SATURDAY: Vanessa left a message on my answering machine in her grating, shrilly voice wondering why I did not show up today. Just hearing her made me want to smash the machine with my fist.

However, I lacked the strength to even use the TV remote and ended up catching eleven straight hours of the Shopping Channel.

SUNDAY: I'm having the Church van pick me up for services today so I can go and thank GOD that this week is over.

I will also pray that next year, my wife (the bitch), will choose a gift for me that is fun -- like a root canal or a vasectomy.

Busy night. The night before the Falcons played the Broncos in the 1999 Super Bowl XXXVIII, Eugene Robinson, a Falcon's safety was arrested for soliciting sex from an undercover Miami police officer.

Eugene did play in that Super Bowl, but during the game, he flatly missed tackling Terrell Davis, and allowed a 39-yard pass, and run.

The funny thing about it was several Denver players remarked, "What's up Eugene, did you have a busy night last night?" and "Up late last night, huh?" And so forth.

Denver won 34-19.

Reflection. "To love the Super Bowl, you only have to think what Januarys were like before it came along."

    -- David N. Rosenthal

Super Bowl locations. Miami has been the location for the most Super Bowls (10) and New Orleans is second with 9.

Oh? You don't believe in me? "Oh, you didn't want to believe in me. Did you say I can't?

"That's OK, because I'll make a believer out of you."

-- Josh Allen. He did make believers out of everyone. After the first two bad seasons, Josh in 2020 led the Bills to their first division title and playoff victory since 1995 and set the Bills franchise records for single-season passing yards and touchdowns, while earning Pro Bowl and second-team All-Pro honors.

I'll show you. "Though I've passed 316 yards there's still two games to go if I want to make it to the Super Bowl and show everyone on Earth how to Tebow."

-- **Tim Tebow**. Tebow played college football at Florida, where he became the first sophomore to win the Heisman Trophy and led his team to two BCS National Championship victories in 2007 and 2009

Life's experiences. "Every experience, good or bad, you have to learn from, and no one really sees pro athletes behind the scenes.

"They don't know how hard they work. They don't see how you work on the basics. They couldn't possibly know.

You wouldn't think that someone who hits like Alex Rodriguez needs to use a tee every day. But that's how he stayed on top of it."

-- **Patrick Mahones.**

Patrick spent his rookie season as the backup to Alex Smith. He was named the starter in 2018 after the Chiefs traded Smith to the Washington Redskins.

That season, Mahomes threw for 5,097 yards, 50 touchdowns, and 12 interceptions. He became the only quarterback in history to throw for over 5,000 yards in a single season in both college and in the NFL.

Patrick and Peyton Manning are the only players in NFL history to throw 50 touchdown passes and 5,000 yards in a single season. [20]

Patrick Mahones

Fire. I was watching the Super Bowl at my friend's house when my real estate agent called me and told me about a large fire in my neighborhood and my property burned down. So, I instantly realized in both cases Mahomes is on fire!

Madden's humility. "If you win a Super Bowl before you're fired, you're a genius, and everyone listens to you. But a coach is just a guy whose best class in grammar school was recess and whose best class in high school was P.E. I never thought I was anything but a guy whose best class was P.E."

-- **John Madden**. John was head coach of the Oakland Raiders from 1969 to 1978. He led them to eight playoff appearances, seven division titles, seven AFL / AFC Championship Game appearances, and the franchise's first Super Bowl title in Super Bowl XI.

He didn't ever have a losing season and holds the highest winning percentage among NFL head coaches who coached 100 games. [21]

Narrowing it down. "We can't run. We can't pass. We can't stop the run. We can't stop the pass. We can't kick. Other than that, we're just not a very good football team right now."

-- **Bruce Coslet**, Former American college and professional football player and professional football coach

Reflection. "Everybody growing up where I came from had a designer shoe. Nobody had Balenciaga's and all the stuff that we walk around in now. If you had Jordans, that was like a prize basically."

-- **Davante Adams**, wide receiver for the Raiders

Lucky beard. "I just forgot to shave, I guess. … I kept my beard for about two-and-a-half, three months. It was more of a superstition thing. We didn't lose ever since I had it, so I wasn't going to go in there and shave it for the Super Bowl."

— **Julian Edelman**, Patriots wide receiver victorious over the Seahawks (Super Bowl XLIX).

Champion. "A champion is simply someone who did not give up when they wanted to."

-- **Tom Landry**, former coach Dallas Cowboys

Why won't Lucy let Charlie Brown kick the football?

Analysis. "No matter how reassured that Lucy won't swipe the football, and no matter how many times she goes back on her word, Charlie chooses to engage in the same behavior, and pays the same price, over and over.

"Charlie is torn between the obligatory trust one should have in a friend, and the foreseeable consequences of trusting Lucy.

"Charlie knows that the first time he tells Lucy he is not going to let her hold the football for him she will loudly protest his distrust, question his friendship and stomp off in a huff.

"Charlie is not willing to risk this outcome. But Charlie is operating on a false paradigm as Lucy is about Lucy and no one else.

"Eventually, Lucy gets so accustomed to pulling the prank without a hint of protest that she eventually forgets that but for Charlie's largesse she would never get away with this kind of anti-social behavior.

"Lucy is a hopeless narcissist and if there's any doubt about that one need only review her record as an ersatz psychiatrist. She doesn't care a lick about her patients; she cares only for her self-exalted status and getting paid.

"Charlie is an enabler of the worst sort. He keeps going back hoping this time will be different but knowing it won't. He may not be responsible for Lucy's narcissistic behavior, but he is responsible for helping turn her into the little tyrant she is."

-- Anonymous psychologist in training.

Another analysis, Lucy is just having fun with blockhead!

Turn it around. "If there's the opportunity to turn things around, that's what great players do. They don't complain or become complacent with losing. They just go back to work every day and try to turn things around and make wherever they are a great place to be."

-- **Myles Garrett**, defensive end Cleveland Browns

Life is like football. "The game of life is a lot like football. You have to tackle your problems, block your fears, and score your points when you get the opportunity."

-- **Lewis Grizzard.** Writer and humorist.

Prove something? "Anytime you come out there and you try to 'prove something,' you're trying to be more than you are."

-- **Cooper Kupp**, wide receiver for the Rams

No coincidence. "Thanksgiving dinners take eighteen hours to prepare. They are consumed in twelve minutes. Half-times take twelve minutes. This is not coincidence."

-- **Erma Bombeck**

Exposing buttocks. "This helicopter flies overhead, probably taking pictures, and McMahon just moons it. He mooned the helicopter from the field."

-- **William "The Refrigerator" Perry** talking about Jim McMahon former Bear QB.

Meaning. "Success comes in a lot of ways, but it doesn't come with money, and it doesn't come with fame.

"It comes from having a meaning in your life, doing what you love, and being passionate about what you do. That's having a life of success.

"When you can do what you love, love what you do and have the ability to impact people, that's having a life of success. That's what having a life of meaning is."

— **Tim Tebow.** Quarterback who also said, *"I can't control the naysayers. I can control my attitude and work ethic and determination and that's what I'm focused on now."* And he also said, *"Strong leaders encourage you to do things for your own benefit, not just theirs."*

Good morning! Sometimes, getting up in the morning and brushing your teeth is the hardest part of the day — it all just hurts.

-- **Tom Brady**

Class. "Self-praise is for losers. Be a winner. Stand for something. Always have class and be humble."

-- **John Madden**

Long medical history. "My knees look like they lost a knife fight with a midget."

-- **E.J. Holub,** Kansas City Chief's Hall of Famer, E. J. Holub, 6-4" - 238 lbs. He played center and linebacker over his 127-game career.

A silent tribute. In 2004, Sean Taylor was a rising NFL star and the No. 5 draft pick by the Redskins.

Previously, he played for the University of Miami on their National Championship Team. He had everything going for him as a young man.

In 2007, his Florida home was invaded by intruders who shot and killed him in his own home.

The entire NFL as well as the Washington team was in shock and provided love, condolences, and support for Sean's family.

The five intruders were caught, convicted, and received prison sentences.

The Redskins played the Buffalo Bills in the next game and the defensive coach and players lined up with only 10 men leaving the place vacant where Sean would play. The player who eventually took Sean's position stood silently on the sideline as a tribute to Sean.

The newspapers reported head coach Joe Gibbs didn't know the defense was going to do this silent tribute to Sean and all felt later that *"It was important for the team to know that Sean was with us that one last time on the field. He'll always be with us, but that was special."*

Did you know this? The record for the most seasons played is 26 held by George Blanda.

Blanda retired from pro football in August 1976 as the oldest player to ever play at the age of 48.

George was one of only two players to play in four different decades (John Carney was the other). George holds the record for most extra points made (943) and attempted extra points (959).

During his career, he played under renowned head coaches Bear Bryant, George Halas, Clem Crowe, Lou Rymkus, Wally Lemm, Pop Ivy, Sammy Baugh, Hugh Taylor, John Rauch, and John Madden. [22]

For a Football Fan Who Has Everything by Bruce Miller & Team Golfwell

The passing of an NFL great. Oakland Raiders owner Al Davis modernized the NFL, and he passed in October 2011 at the age of 82.

The next day, the Raiders held a moment in silence for Al, and a day later, the Raiders played a road game against the Houston Texans and trailed with not much time remaining until safety Michael Huff intercepted Matt Schaub's pass and resulting in a win for Oakland.

Head coach Hue Jackson sank to one knee and cried along with many of the players as a tribute to Al.

Michael Huff told reporters, "We know he's looking down on us right now. This win is for him. I appreciate everything he's done for this organization. He's never gone in our eyes. We'll never let him go. He's with us."

Most points scored. The record for the most points scored in a career is held by kicker, Adam Vinatieri with 2,673 points in 24 seasons with the New England Patriots and the Indianapolis Colts. [23]

The longest…game time. The longest game of all time happened back in 1971 on Christmas Day when the Dolphins defeated the Chiefs, 27-24, in sudden-death overtime in an AFC Divisional Playoff game.

The game time ended with the teams tied 24-24. After passing the two-minute and 54-second mark in double overtime, the game broke the record for the longest game time in NFL history.

The game would go on for roughly five more minutes and ended when Garo Yepremian kicked a 37-yard field goal to give the Dolphins the victory.

In total, the matchup lasted a game time of 82 minutes and 40 seconds, making it the longest game in NFL history. [24]

An old one. An NFL coach and his assistant were looking at a roster when one of them came across an unusual name.

"Quasimodo? Why does that name ring a bell?"

His assistant replied, "He was at Notre Dame... a halfback."

Dad joke. Q. What did the wide receiver say to the football after he missed it?

A. "Catch you later."

Say what? "I'm the football coach around here and don't you remember it."

-- **Bill Peterson.** (1920 -1993) Former professional football player who played linebacker for five seasons for the Cincinnati Bengals one season with Kansas City Chiefs and one season with New England Patriots, and coached Houston Oilers.

It's truly the people. "I wanted to really ingrain myself in the culture and the people. And I apologize about having an allergy to dairy products that gives me some irritable bowels, but other than that, I mean, I've embraced just about everything else Wisconsin - especially when it comes to sports, but also the people and the interactions with our fans."

-- **Aaron Rodgers.** It's been said it's best always to be yourself unless you can become Aaron Rodgers…Then always be Aaron Rodgers.

In April 2018, Aaron became a limited partner in the Milwaukee Bucks ownership group, making him the first active NFL player with an ownership stake in an NBA franchise

Ironhead. Craig "Ironhead" Heyward was a fullback who played for the Pitt Panthers in College, New Orleans Saints, Chicago Bears, Atlanta Falcons, St. Louis Rams, and Indianapolis Colts in an 11-year National Football League (NFL) career.

He is at times unfortunately known for his statement before the NFL draft, when he told a reporter, *"People say I'll be drafted in the first round, maybe even higher."*

According to his son, Cameron Heyward, a defensive lineman for the Pittsburgh Steelers, his father got his nickname, "Ironhead" when he was 12 or 13 years old. He was at the Boys & Girls Club in Passaic, New Jersey.

Another boy approached him and broke a pool cue over Craig's head. Craig barely flinched, and his grandmother called him "Ironhead," and the nickname stuck. [25]

Unknown brother. "Nobody in football should be called a genius. A genius is a guy like Norman Einstein."

-- **Joe Theismann**. Quarterback. Joe Theismann's last name is actually pronounced as "Theeseman", but he changed the pronunciation before beginning his senior year at Notre Dame because it rhymes with Heisman. Joe explained this over the phone on the Dan Patrick show. [26]

Theismann said Roger Valdiserri, Notre Dame's Sports Information Director at the time, approached him and told him that he was to change the pronunciation of his last name because it rhymes with Heisman, and that made for a better Heisman campaign.

And that's the pronunciation commonly used to this day. [27]

He was fierce. "When I played football, I never set out to hurt anybody deliberately unless it was, you know, important, like a league game or something."

-- **Dick Butkus,** Hall of Famer Middle Linebacker. (Chicago Bears). Also said, *"My shoulder surgery was a success. The lobotomy failed."*

Largest attended game (so far). Everything is big in Texas, right? The largest season crowd in NFL history was the 2009 Game at AT&T Stadium on September 20 in Arlington, Texas. ***The Cowboys and Giants drew 105,121 fans.*** [28]

Determination. "The harder you work, the harder it is to surrender."

    -- **Marv Levy**, Former Coach Buffalo Bills.

Free. "I can honestly tell you I would play this game for free."

    -- **Troy Palamalu**, former safety for the Steelers. Polamalu is an eight-time Pro Bowler.

Bart Starr's father. "My father - who was a master sergeant and the toughest man I've even known - next to him, Coach Lombardi was a piece of cake."

Ben Starr, Bart's father, was a career non-commissioned officer in the Air Force, and some say his military background clearly played a crucial role in building the fortitude and inner strength that would allow Bart to stand up and develop well under the ever-demanding pressure of Coach Lombardi.

That discipline lasted Bart's whole life.

Bart Starr

Dealing with it. "Life is 10% what happens to you, and 90% how you respond to it."

-- **Lou Holtz**. Player, coach, and analyst. He coached various major college and university teams and most of his career coaching Notre Dame (1986–1996).

He also coached the University of South Carolina (1999–2004) and had a total career record of 249–132–7.

At Notre Dame in 1988, his team went 12–0 with a final victory in the Fiesta Bowl. Most sportswriters agreed that was a national championship team.

Lou is the only college football coach to lead six different programs to bowl games and the only coach to guide four different programs to the final top 20 rankings. He went on to be an analyst for CBS Sports and ESPN.

Lou Holtz

"Success isn't owned. It's leased. But my rent is due every day."

-- **J. J. Watt**. Former defensive end for the Arizona Cardinals.

For a Football Fan Who Has Everything by Bruce Miller & Team Golfwell

J. J. Watt

On failures and wins – Coach Bum Phillips.

"You fail all the time. But you aren't a failure until you start blaming someone else."

"The only discipline that lasts, is self-discipline."

"How do you win? By getting average players to play good and good players to play great. That's how you win."

"Coaching is not how much you know. It's how much you can get players to do."

-- **Bum Phillips**, former coach, Houston Texans

Bum Phillips

What it is. "If you're not in the parade, you watch the parade. That's life."

-- **Mike Ditka**, Former Player and Coach (Chicago Bears). He is one of only two men to have won a Super Bowl as a player, assistant coach and head coach. Ditka is also one of only four head coaches to record more than 100 victories in only 10 seasons.

Charger defense. "Bobby Tom told me he's not afraid of the Chargers' defense. Bobby Tomb will tell you he's not afraid of nuclear war, so I wouldn't put too much stock in his opinion."

— **Susan Elizabeth Phillips**, It Had to Be You

How I started. "This is how I started playing: I was playing hooky one day, and the coach and the principal walked up behind me. They scared me, and I ran, and they noticed I could run really fast. They wanted me to come out for the football team."

-- **Jerry Rice.** Widely considered to be the greatest wide receiver in NFL history. He has also said, *"Today I will do what others won't, so tomorrow I can accomplish what others can't."*

Contacting Tech Support

Dear Tech Support,

Last year I upgraded from Boyfriend 5.0 to Husband 1.0 and noticed a distinct slowdown in overall system performance --

particularly in the flower and jewelry applications, which operated flawlessly under Boyfriend 5.0.

In addition, Husband 1.0 uninstalled many other valuable programs, such as Romance 9.5 and Personal Attention 6.5 and then installed undesirable programs such as **NFL 5.0**, NBA 3.0, and Golf Clubs 4.1. Conversation 8.0 no longer runs and Housecleaning 2.6 simply crashes the system. I've tried running Nagging 5.3 to fix these problems, but to no avail.

What can I do?

Signed,

"Desperate Football Widow"

Tech Support reply.

Dear Desperate,

First, keep in mind, that Boyfriend 5.0 is an Entertainment Package, while Husband 1.0 is an Operating System.

Please enter the command "! http: I Thought You Loved Me.html" and try to download Tears 6.2 and don't forget to install the Guilt 3.0 update. If that application works as designed, Husband 1.0 should then automatically run the applications Jewelry 2.0 and Flowers 3.5.

But remember, overuse of the above application can cause Husband 1.0 to default to Grumpy Silence 2.5, Happy Hour 7.0

For a Football Fan Who Has Everything by Bruce Miller & Team Golfwell

or Beer 6.1. Beer 6.1 is a very bad program that will download the Snoring Loudly Beta.

Whatever you do, DO NOT install Mother-in-law 1.0 (it runs a virus in the background that will eventually seize control of all your system resources). Also, do not attempt to reinstall the Boyfriend 5.0 program. These are unsupported applications and will crash Husband 1.0.

In summary, Husband 1.0 is a great program, but it does have limited memory and cannot learn new applications quickly. You might consider buying additional software to improve memory and performance. We recommend! Food 3.0 and Hot Lingerie 7.7.

Good Luck,

Tech Support

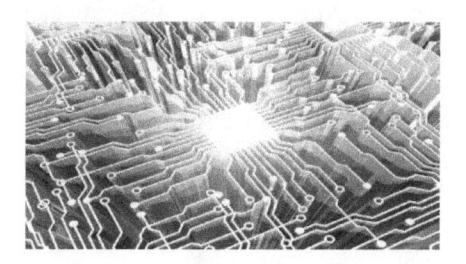

What work really is. "Work isn't work unless you would rather be doing something else."

-- **Don Shula**, Former highly renowned Coach, Miami Dolphins. Don is the NFL's winningest head coach at 347 career victories and 328 regular season victories.

He held his first head coaching position with the Baltimore Colts, whom he led for seven seasons, and spent his next 26 seasons with Miami.

Shula had only two losing seasons during his 33 years as a head coach and led the Dolphins to two consecutive Super Bowl titles in Super Bowl VII and Super Bowl VIII.

His first Super Bowl title in 1972 is the only perfect season in NFL history. [29]

What do rich people buy, Jimmy? Defensive end, J. J. Watt asked Jimmy Kimmel while being on his show that question.

J.J told Jimmy he had to Google "What do rich people buy" since he didn't really know, and he just signed a $100-million contract in 2011.

Makes you think, doesn't it?

Turns out J. J. said he held off buying anything since all the stuff seemed extravagant, unnecessary, and over the top to him.

For a Football Fan Who Has Everything by Bruce Miller & Team Golfwell

Practice. "For every pass I caught in a game, I caught a 1000 in practice."

-- **Don Hutson**, Former receiver, Green Bay Packers

No promises. "Remember, today is today and tomorrow is promised to no one."

-- **Walter Payton**, Former running back Chicago Bears and regarded as one of the greatest football players of all time.

Payton set records during his time and retired with the most receptions by a non-receiver, and he had caught eight career touchdown passes.

Tough Exam. (This joke was donated by a Bear fan) Two Green Bay Packer football players, Bubba and Tiny, were taking an important exam when they were in college to keep their eligibility to play college football before they turned pro. If they failed, they would be on academic probation and not allowed to play in a big college bowl and perhaps not even make the pros.

The exam was "fill in the blank" and the last question read, "Old MacDonald had a____."

Bubba was stumped -- he had no idea what to answer, but he knew he needed to get this one right to be sure he passed.

Making sure the teacher wasn't watching, he tapped Tiny on the shoulder. "Tiny, what's the answer to the last question?"

Tiny laughed, then looked around to make sure the professor hadn't noticed. He turned to Bubba and said, "Bubba, you're so stupid. Everyone knows that Old MacDonald had a FARM."

"Oh yeah," said Bubba, "I remember now." he picked up his No. 2 pencil and started to write the answer in the blank. Then he stopped. Tapping Tiny on the shoulder, he whispered, "Tiny, how do you spell farm?"

"You are really dumb, Bubba. that's so easy," hissed Tiny, "farm is spelled E-I-E-I-O.'"

This is how you play. "You have to play this game like somebody just hit your mother with a two-by-four."

    -- **Dan Birdwell**, Defensive lineman. He played collegiately for the University of Houston and professionally for the Oakland Raiders of the American Football League from 1962 to 1969.

Keep on keeping on! "Don't worry about the horse being blind, just load the wagon"

-- **John Madden** who said, *"This is one of my favorite all time quotes. I use it often and people look at me quizzically when I do. In coach speak, it means, just keep plugging and don't worry about what's going on around you."*

"The thing about football - the important thing about football - is that it is not just about football."

— **Terry Pratchett**, Unseen Academicals

Wives. "I love being in the room with my husband while he eats, cheers, burps, shouts, completely ignores me and watches football – said no wife ever."

-- Anon.

The Oldest Rivalry. Chicago Bears and Green Bay Packers are the oldest rivalry in Professional football going back over a hundred years to 1921. [30]

It started on November 27, 1921, when the Bears shut out the Packers 20-0. NFL founder **George Halas** caught a 10-yard pass from **Chic Harley**. During that game, there was a large brawl where Chicago's **John "Tarzan" Taylor** beat up **Howard Buck** breaking his nose and the long rivalry began.

For a Football Fan Who Has Everything by Bruce Miller & Team Golfwell

Getting ahead. "Winning isn't getting ahead of others. It's getting ahead of yourself."

-- **Roger Staubach**, Dallas Cowboys

Roger Staubach

Go for it. "If you're not gonna go ALL the way, why go at ALL?"

-- "Broadway" **Joe Namath**, New York Jets

The enemy of the best. "The Enemy of the best is the good. If you're always settling with what's good, you'll never be the best."

— Jerry Rice

"I do that too with my assistant." During the deflated ball (Deflategate) scandal, Rams defensive end, Chris Long joked about Tom Brady destroying his cell phone and said he tends to do the same, when he is with his assistant.

"My assistant Jack Daniels and I actually destroy a cell phone every four months or so."

Two things. "Football combines two of the worst things in American life. It is violence punctuated by committee meetings."

— **George Will**, Columnist for the Washington Post

Stand by me. "Anyone can support a team that is winning - it takes no courage. But to stand behind a team to defend a team when it is down and really needs you, that takes a lot of courage."

For a Football Fan Who Has Everything by Bruce Miller & Team Golfwell

-- **Bart Starr**

Intriguing questions.

Q. Can you name the 3 NFL team's mascots that start with the letter "F"?

A. The Falcons, the Forty-Niners, and the F***ing Dolphins!

Q. What's the difference between an NFL player and a soccer player?

A. When you pat an NFL player on the shoulder, they feel better. But the other gets hospitalized right away.

Q. Did you hear about the first female NFL referee?

A. She threw a flag for something that happened last season.

They're just grown up now. "The same boys who got detention in elementary school for beating the crap out of people are now rewarded for it. They call it football."

― **Laurie Halse Anderson**, Speak

Could be anyone. "The next MVP of the Super Bowl is just as likely to have been a full-time grocery store bagger last year as a Heisman Trophy winner."

    -- **Hunter S. Thompson**

Talk to the best. "I got to talk with some of the great offensive minds in football. Bruce Arians, Byron Leftwich, Andy Reid, Ben McAdoo, Bill O'Brien, I met all those guys and tried to take something away from each of them.

"Hue Jackson and people that are known for developing quarterbacks, I got exposed to a lot of stuff I hadn't seen before."

    -- **Patrick Mahomes II**

College team banter.

Q. How many Alabama freshmen does it take to change a light bulb?

A. None. That's a sophomore course.

Q: Why is Alabama college football so strong?

A: Because they're all one big family.

Q: When you put 32 Arkansas cheerleaders together, what do you have?

A: A full set of teeth.

Q: A genius sitting in the Texas A&M student section will be called what?

A: A visitor.

Q: Why do Corn Husker football players like smart women?

A: Opposites attract.

Q. What do you have when you put 32 Arkansas cheerleaders together?

A. A full set of teeth.

For a Football Fan Who Has Everything by Bruce Miller & Team Golfwell

Q. How do you get a Texas A&M player off your front steps?

A. Pay him for the pizza.

Q. Why is the Vanderbilt football team like a possum?

A. Because they play dead at home and get killed on the road.

Q. Why did Tennessee choose orange as their team color?

A. You can wear it to the game on Saturday, hunting on Sunday, and picking up trash along the highways the rest of the week.

Q: How would you know if a Georgia football player has a girlfriend?

A: You would see tobacco juice on both sides of his F-150.

Q: How do you get a Texas A&M player off your front step?

A: Pay him for the pizza.

Meaning of luck. "Sure, luck means a lot in football. Not having a good quarterback is bad luck."

    -- **Don Shula**

Dad joke. Q. What do you call a boat full of polite football players?

A. Good sportsman ship.

An old one. "It's not the size of the dog in the fight, but the size of the fight in the dog."

    -- **Archie Griffin**, Cincinnati Bengals

Father of American Football. Football has origins going back to Ancient Greece, where men played a similar sport called "Episkyros" where they tried to throw a ball over a scrimmage while avoiding tackles, and later sports known as mob football and others such as rugby.

Early evidence of football - A bottle in gnathic style depicting a figure playing with a ball, third quarter of the 4th century BCE

Walter Camp is considered by most to be the "Father of American football" as he instituted rules "that a team be required to advance the ball a minimum of five yards within three downs. These down-and-distance rules, combined with the establishment of the line of scrimmage and forward pass, transformed the game from a variation of rugby football into the distinct sport and football code of American football." [31]

Camp established four points for a touchdown, two points for kicks after touchdowns, two points for safeties, and five for field goals. By the way, a safety is unique to American football as there is no similar rule in rugby.

Camp established game time for two halves of 45 minutes each and there be two officials, a referee and an umpire, and the officials were given whistles and stopwatches.

Finally, and this is what makes American football unique, he made blocking legal (which is illegal in rugby).

Blocking was created by Camp when he coached his Yale team when the opposing team found creative ways of aiding the runner by pretending to accidentally knock into defenders trying to tackle the runner.

When Walter Camp witnessed this phony tactic, he was at first appalled, but the next year had adopted the blocking tactics for his own team.

Later, during the 1880s and 1890s, teams developed increasingly complex blocking tactics including the interlocking interference technique known as the Flying wedge or "V-trick formation" which was developed by **Lorin F. Deland** and introduced by Harvard in a collegiate game against Yale in 1892.

Despite its effectiveness, it was outlawed two seasons later in 1894 due to serious injuries. [32]

In the present day, the Walter Camp Football Foundation continues to select All-American teams in his honor.

Good idea. "The easiest way to remember your future wife's birthday is to marry her on Super Bowl Sunday."

-- **Matshona Dhliwayo**, Canadian based Philosopher, Entrepreneur, and author

For a Football Fan Who Has Everything by Bruce Miller & Team Golfwell

Sharks. "Sharks are as tough as those football fans who take their shirts off during games in Chicago in January, only more intelligent."

-- **Dave Barry,** author, columnist, and humorist.

Stones. An avid football fan appeared in court one day charged with disorderly conduct and assault. The arresting officer stated that the accused had thrown something into the river.

Judge: "What exactly did the accused throw?"

Officer: "Stones, sir."

Judge: "Well, that's hardly an offense is it?"

Officer: It was in this case, sir. Mr. Stones was the referee."

Blindsided. "You get hit the hardest when trying to run or hide from a problem. Like the defense on a football field, putting all focus on evading only one defender is asking to be blindsided."

— **Criss Jami**, Killosophy

Only Bradshaw could say this. "I may be dumb, but I'm not stupid."

-- **Terry Bradshaw.** Former renowned Steelers quarterback and TV personality. There's only one Terry Bradshaw. In 1983, he used Tom Brady's name when he checked into a hospital for minor elbow surgery. Terry said, *"When I woke up after the operation, a doctor came into the room and told me they had used an alias, so I'd be able to rest without being bothered. He said, 'Your name's 'Thomas Brady.' That's how it happened."* [33]

Brett Favre's first-ever NFL completion. The first pass completion (so to speak) by the highly regarded quarterback Brett Favre, was actually to himself, because on his first pass (Sept 13, 1992) the ball bounced off a Tampa Bay Bucs defender's helmet, flew up in the air, and Brett caught it unfortunately for a seven-yard loss. [34]

Brett went on to complete 22 passes and led his team to a 24-23 victory over the Bucs. [35]

For a Football Fan Who Has Everything by Bruce Miller & Team Golfwell

Brett Favre

Brett's father, Irvin, died suddenly at age 58 in 2003. Hesitant and undecided whether he should play the next day on Monday Night Football. He did play and he beat the Raiders with four touchdowns and passed for a game total of 311 yards.

In an interview afterward, he told reporters, *"I knew that my dad would have wanted me to play. I love him so much, and I love this game. It's meant a great deal to me, to my dad, to my family, and I didn't expect this kind of performance. But I know he was watching tonight."*

Turn the TV on and get a beer. "I like football. I find it's an exciting strategic game. It's a great way to avoid conversation with your family at Thanksgiving."

— **Craig Ferguson**, Actor, and comedian.

Necessities -- When you gotta go. Miami Dolphins' **Channing Crowder** talked about what he does when nature calls and you are in front of thousands of people.

He said you just go he did just that in every single NFL game he played in. *"I would just be in the huddle, just pee, like you wouldn't even ... nobody in the stands would know unless you looked down like 'That ... That's not water, man!'* [36]

Carolina Panther's center, **Ryan Kalil** said, *"Guys are peeing all over the sideline in every game, into cups, on the ground, in towels, behind the bench, in their pants, everywhere."* [37]

The shape of a football. Originally, the football was larger and rounder. But in 1934, the shape was made narrower to promote the passing game.

Pro teams' banter.

Q: What was the result of the joke that **Carson Wentz** told his receivers?

A: It went over their heads.

Q: How can you keep the Detroit Lions out of your front yard?

A: By putting up a goal post.

Q: Do you know the difference between the Dallas Cowboys and a dollar bill?

A: You can still get four quarters from a dollar bill.

Q: Why do 49ers fans smell so bad?

A: So that blind people can hate them as well.

Q: In case of a tornado, where should you go for safety in Chicago?

A: Soldier Field - they never get a touchdown there!

Jim Brown. "The only way to stop Jim Brown was to give him a movie contract."

Jim Brown 6'2" and 232 lbs. was an amazing fullback, sports analyst, and actor. He played for the Cleveland Browns from 1957 through 1965. [38] Jim is thought of by many to be one of the greatest running backs of all time, as well as one of the greatest players in the NFL. And surprisingly still holds the NFL records for,

- Most games with 24 or more points in a career (6)

- Highest career touchdowns per game average (1.068)

- Most games with four or more touchdowns in a career (6)

- Most seasons leading the league in rushing yards (8)

- Highest career rushing yards-per-game average (104.3)

- Most seasons leading the league in touchdowns (5)

- Highest average yards from scrimmage per game in a career (125.52 yds.)

In 1975, He was convicted of misdemeanor battery for beating and choking his golfing partner, Frank Snow. He was sentenced to one day in jail, probation, and a fine of $500. [39] Many golfers can understand that especially when they talk during your backswing – Just kidding!

Jim Brown

Second place isn't bad. The Buffalo Bills in the early 1990s lost four straight Super Bowls in a row. The Vikings also have lost four Super Bowls. Both the Bills and the Vikings haven't ever won a Super Bowl.

Denver also lost four Super Bowls, but unlike the Bills or the Vikings, the Broncos have won two Super Bowls.

Players get bonuses (in addition to their regular pay) for playing in the Super Bowl. In 2022, the winning players got $150,000 while the losers got $75,000 each.

The Steelers and the Patriots hold the record for the most Super Bowl wins with 6 wins each. The Forty-Niners have won the Super Bowl 5 times and only lost once to

Team effort. "I don't see why there is any reason to pick out one individual as the MVP because it is about a team winning a championship."

-- **Jim Nantz,** Sportscaster.

Would you rather? "I'd rather have 10 Super Bowl trophies and no MVPs."

-- **Justin Tuck**, a college football player at Notre Dame, and was drafted by the New York Giants in the third round of the 2005 Draft.

He played defensive end and was instrumental in winning two Super Bowl titles with the team, both against the New England Patriots.

Intimidation by osmosis. "The first thing that came to mind when I met Tom Brady was intimidation. I'm showing up in 2005 with a guy who just came off his third Super Bowl win. So, it's a little intimidating walking in the room with Tom Brady for the first time."

-- **Matt Cassel**, Former American football quarterback who played in the National Football League for 14 seasons.

Who does Tom Brady look up to? "Who's my hero? That's a great question... Well, I think my dad is my hero, because he's someone I look up to every day."

Tom Brady Sr. founded his own insurance firm, Thomas Brady and Associates, located in San Francisco, with offices in Boston and New York.

Tom Sr. and his wife had a family policy that their children (3 daughters and Tom, Jr.) could do whatever they wanted to do and instilled a spirit of competition in them. Seems they did a great job!

An old one. On the first day of school in the northern suburbs of Chicago, a first-grade teacher explains to her class that she is a Bears fan. She asks her students to raise their hands if they, too, are Bears fans.

Wanting to impress their teacher, everyone in the class raises their hand except one little girl. The teacher looks at the girl with surprise, 'Janie, why didn't you raise your hand?'

Because I'm not a Bears fan,' she replied.

The teacher, still shocked, asked, 'Well, if you are not a Bears fan, then who are you a fan of?'

'I am a Packers fan, and proud of it,' Janie replied.

The teacher could not believe her ears. 'Janie please tell us why you are a Packers fan?'

"Because my mom is a Packers fan, and my dad is Packer's fan, so I'm a Packers fan too!"

"Well," said the teacher in an annoyed tone, 'That is no reason for you to be a Packers fan. You don't have to be just like your parents all of the time. What if your mom was an idiot and your dad was a moron, what would you be then?'

"Then," Janie smiled, "I'd be a Bears fan."

More pro banter.

Q: A Raiders fan and a bottle of beer have what in common?

A: Both are empty from the neck up.

Q: What is the difference between a Dallas Cowboys fan and a baby?

A: The baby will stop whining after a while.

Q: When you cross two football teams with the Invisible Man, what do you get?

A: A game of football like you've never seen.

100% "Most football players are temperamental. That's 90 percent temper and 10 percent mental."

-- **Doug Plank**, Former hard-hitting Chicago Bear safety and later coach.

Mental toughness. "Every quarterback can throw a ball; every running back can run; every receiver is fast; but that mental toughness that you talk about translates into competitiveness."

-- **Tom Brady**

No way. "Cancel the Super Bowl? That's like canceling Christmas!"

-- **Thomas Harris**. Writer and novelist.

Rugby. As a Brit, I can't get into American football, They rugby the wrong way.

Comparison. "American football makes rugby look like a Tupperware party."

-- Sue Lawley, English TV presenter.

NFL record for most touchdowns. Jerry Rice holds the record for the most touchdowns – 208.

— **Jerry Rice** once said to a reporter praising him while Jerry was trying to be modest, *"I feel like I'm the best, but you're not going to get me to say that."*

For a Football Fan Who Has Everything by Bruce Miller & Team Golfwell

Turn me down?

Q. What did the NFL Commissioner say when Adele turned down the Superbowl Halftime Show?

A. "Never mind, I'll find someone like you."

Peyton Manning goes to heaven.
Peyton Manning, after living a full life, died. When he got to heaven, God was showing him around. They came to a modest little house with a faded Colts flag in the window. "This house is yours for eternity, Peyton," said God. "This is very special; not everyone gets a house up here."

Peyton felt special, indeed, and walked up to his house. On his way up the sidewalk, he noticed another house just around the corner. It was a 3-story mansion with a blue and red sidewalk, a 50-foot-tall flagpole with an enormous Patriots logo flag, and in every window hung a red Patriots towel and a few had Tampa Bay towels.

Peyton looked at God and said "God, I'm not trying to be ungrateful, but I have a question. I was an all-pro QB, I hold many NFL records, and I even went to the Hall of Fame."

"So, what's your point Peyton?", God asked.

"Well, why does Tom Brady get a better house than me?"

God chuckled, and replied, "Peyton, that's not Tom's house, it's mine."

No, not another one of those meetings! "Football combines two of the worst things in American life. It is violence punctuated by committee meetings."

— **George Will**, political commentator and author.

First Afro-American. Charles W. Follis, also known as "The Black Cyclone," (1879–1910) was the first Black professional American football player. He played for the Shelby Blues of the "Ohio League" from 1902 to 1906. On September 16, 1904, Follis signed a contract with Shelby making him the first Black man contracted to play professional football on an integrated team. [40]

Charles' role as the first Black professional football player was not known by sports historians until 1975 when researchers rediscovered halfback Follis' on-the-field-achievements while reviewing old pages of the Shelby Daily Globe.

After hours of examining the tattered newspapers, researchers finally came across an article in the September 16, 1904, edition that announced Follis had signed a contract for the upcoming season. [41]

For a Football Fan Who Has Everything by Bruce Miller & Team Golfwell

Charles W. Follis, Wikipedia

What's really important. "It's ridiculous for a country to get all worked up about a game—except the Super Bowl, of course. Now that's important."

-- **Andy Rooney**. Radio and TV Personality.

For a Football Fan Who Has Everything by Bruce Miller & Team Golfwell

Legendary team. A Catholic High School had a legendary football team. Every year, the team was in the state championship game, and usually won it handily. Every able lad within a few hundred miles wanted to play football for Central Catholic Fighting Knights.

Those who were familiar with the program knew that the true heart and soul of the Knights football program was Sister Mary Margaret, an aged nun who would, in full habit, get out on the practice field and work on routes with the receivers, give pointers to the quarterbacks on their stances and releases, but most of all, love them like the second mother that she became to all of the boys in that program.

One year, on the eve of the state championship game, some evil malefactors broke into the convent and kidnapped Sister Mary Margaret. Everyone was stunned by the news, but none more so than the Knights of Central Catholic. They were devastated at the loss of their mentor.

As you might guess, the state championship game didn't go very well. For the first time in the history of the football program, the Knights were shut out. The Spartans beat them 42-0.

The next day, the headline on the local sports section read:

No Offense, Nun Taken.

Don't give up. "A champion is simply someone who did not give up when they wanted to."

-- **Tom Landry**, former Coach - Dallas Cowboys

Are NFL players big? This one certainly was big. Six feet three inches tall and 335 lbs., **William "The Refrigerator" Perry**, former Bears defensive tackle remarked to a reporter, *"I've been big ever since I was little."*

He had a 22 " neck and a size 58 coat when he played and could run a 40 yd. dash in 5.1 seconds. In high school, he ran 100 yards in under 11 seconds.

Female referees. "I just learned the NFL has a female referee. I doubt it very much, but I'm just wondering…"

"Wondering what?"

"When she throws a flag and just stares at a player, and he is supposed to know what he did wrong?

Winter sports. "The problem with winter sports is that -- follow me closely here -- they generally take place in winter."

— **Dave Barry,** Author, columnist, and humorist.

Lack of talent doesn't matter. "A lot of times I find that people who are blessed with the most talent don't ever develop that attitude, and the ones who aren't blessed in that way are the most competitive and have the biggest heart."

-- Tom Brady

Grilled cheese. One of the hottest NFL games involved the Packers (who normally play in freezing weather) and the Arizona Cardinals in week 3 of 2003.

It was 102° F at kickoff and reached up to 106° F by the fourth quarter. Most say this is one of the hottest games in NFL history. [42]

Packer QB **Brett Favre** had a record of 35-1 in games colder than 34°F and 12-18 in games above 70°F.

There were signs in the stands of the crowd teasing Packer "Cheeseheads" like "We'll have the grilled cheese!"

Brett had to deal with safety **Dexter Jackson**, the previous year's Super Bowl XXXVII MVP who intercepted a Favre pass in the fourth quarter sealing an Arizona won 20-13. [43]

Emergency! Sammy was your less-than-average NFL player. He always managed to land on a roster, but in 13 years had never felt the glory of playing on Sunday and always sat on the bench.

Despite being benched all the time, he'd put on his gear, smear his cheeks with eye-black, don his helmet and rush onto the field with his teammates. But play after play, game after game, year after year, he sat on the bench.

One Sunday morning near the end of his lackluster career, Sammy was feeling sick. "Cathy," he asked his wife, "Would you do me a favor?"

"What?" She asked.

"Dress up in my uniform, smear your face, put on my helmet and ride the bench for me today. Nobody will know, and I'm headed for the deer in the woods."

Cathy reluctantly agreed, and sure enough, no one knew Sammy wasn't there. The first three-quarters of the game were uneventful, but in the fourth-quarter, Sammy's team suffered a rash of serious injuries. With no one left on the bench, the coach yelled, "Sammy, get in there!"

Trembling, Cathy ran onto the field, crouched down at the line of scrimmage, and was knocked cold just after the ball was snapped. When she came to, the coach had one hand pushing hard on her breast and the other was between her legs.

"Don't worry, Sammy!" he said nervously. "Once we get your testicles back in place, your manhood will pop right out!"

Giant Riddle. Why is MetLife Stadium the windiest stadium in the NFL?

A. Because there's a Giant fan in every seat.

Largest and smallest NFL Stadiums. The MetLife Stadium, home of the New York Giants and New York Jets is the largest with a seating capacity of 82,500. There was an instance of someone letting a black cat on the field during a game. That took place shortly after Halloween.

Soldier Field, home of the Chicago Bears has the smallest capacity with 61,500. [44]

There have been rumors the NFL is considering having their teams play to empty stadiums and no fans. Some say the Jaguars have been preparing for that their whole lives.

It's halftime in America. "It's halftime. Both teams are in their locker room discussing what they can do to win this game in the second half.

"It's halftime in America, too. People are out of work and they're hurting. And they're all wondering what they're going to do to make a comeback. And we're all scared because this isn't a game.

"The people of Detroit know a little something about this. They almost lost everything. But we all pulled together, now Motor City is fighting again.

"I've seen a lot of tough eras, a lot of downturns in my life. And times when we didn't understand each other. It seems like we've lost our heart at times. When the fog of division, discord, and blame made it hard to see what lies ahead.

"But after those trials, we all rallied around what was right, and acted as one. Because that's what we do. We find a way through tough times, and if we can't find a way, then we'll make one.

"All that matters now is what's ahead. How do we come from behind? How do we come together? And how do we win?

"Detroit's showing us it can be done. And, what's true about them is true about all of us.

"This country can't be knocked out with one punch. We get right back up again and when we do the world is going to hear the roar of our engines.

"Yeah, it's halftime America. And our second half is about to begin."

    -- **Clint Eastwood**, Actor.

The Sunday checklist.

- Put on Jersey.
- Get snacks.
- Get cooler of beer.
- Get on couch.
- Don't move from TV.

Largest American Football Stadium. "Michigan Stadium, nicknamed "The Big House," is the football stadium for the University of Michigan in Ann Arbor, Michigan. It is the largest stadium in the United States and the Western Hemisphere, the third largest stadium in the world, and the 34th largest sports venue in the world. Its official capacity is 107,601 but has hosted crowds of more than 115,000. [45]

University of Michigan Stadium

By the way, the largest stadium in the world is a cricket stadium in India. The Narendra Modi Stadium (formerly: Sardar Vallabhbhai Patel Cricket Stadium) is the largest in the world and is located inside the Sardar Vallabhbhai Patel Sports Enclave in Ahmedabad, India.

As of 2022, it is the largest stadium in the world, with a seating capacity of 132,000 spectators. [46]

The Narendra Modi Stadium (formerly: Sardar Vallabhbhai Patel Cricket Stadium

"We're going to score!" In the 2003-04 playoffs, Seattle played the Packers in Lambeau field. It was an even game as both teams came into it with records of 10-6.

After 4 quarters, the game was tied at 27 each so they went into overtime.

Seattle's **Matt Hasselbeck** was a captain at the coin toss and won the toss and strangely said, *"We want the ball and we're going to score!"*

It seemed Matt was playing overly excited and that backfired since on the first possession by Seahawks, Matt threw an interception to Packer defender **Al Harris** who returned it 52 yards for a touchdown to seal the game.

Seems there is a lot of truth in the saying, *"Don't talk, just act. Don't say, just show. Don't promise, just prove."*

Winning the Super Bowl. "If you win a Super Bowl before you're fired, you're a genius, and everyone listens to you."

>   -- **John Madden**

No necks. "Football practice -- where men are men and necks are nothing."

>   -- **Sam Taylor**

Thinking positive. After a 4-12 losing season, NY Jets quarterback **Geno Smith** told a reporter, *"It's almost exciting to think about all the room for improvement that we have."*

For a Football Fan Who Has Everything by Bruce Miller & Team Golfwell

Geno Smith

It's no accident. "No one wins the Super Bowl accidentally. Be intentional, be passionate, don't mail it in! You got this!"

— **Dave Ramsey**, personal finance personality, radio show host, author, and businessman. An evangelical Christian, host of the nationally syndicated radio program "The Ramsey Show."

Vince Lombardi. Some say he was the greatest coach that ever lived. During the 1960s, he led the Green Bay Packers to three straight and five total NFL Championships in seven years. He also had the first two Super Bowl victories at the end of the 1966 and 1967 NFL seasons. [47]

- He never had a losing season as head coach in the NFL and had a regular-season winning percentage of 73.8% (96–34–6), and 90% (9–1) in the postseason for an overall record of 105 wins, 35 losses and 6 ties in the NFL. [48]

- The year after his sudden death from cancer in 1970, he was enshrined in the Pro Football Hall of Fame, and the NFL Super Bowl trophy was named in his honor.

- Coach Vince Lombardi has said many famous lines over his illustrious career.

- He wasn't ever considered racist during what some consider very racist times. He didn't view his players as being black or white as all to him were "Packer green."

Here a just a few of things he's said during his lifetime,

- "If it doesn't matter who wins or loses, then why do they keep score."

- "Football is like life - it requires perseverance, self-denial, hard work, sacrifice, dedication and respect for authority."

- "Winning is not everything--but making the effort to win is."

- "We didn't lose the game; we just ran out of time."

- "We would accomplish many more things if we did not think of them as impossible."

- "Perfection is not attainable, but if we chase perfection we can catch excellence."

- "There's no substitute for work. "The only place success comes before work is in the dictionary."

- "Football isn't a contact sport; it's a collision sport. Dancing is a contact sport."

- "Once you learn to quit, it becomes a habit."

- "It's not whether you get knocked down, it's whether you get up."

- "I firmly believe that any man's finest hour, the greatest fulfillment of all that he holds dear, is that moment when he has worked his heart out in a good cause and lies exhausted on the field of battle - victorious."

For a Football Fan Who Has Everything by Bruce Miller & Team Golfwell

Vince Lombardi

"It's not that hard to be good. You can be good off raw talent. But I feel like it's that extra step, doing work and putting a body of work in and doing things when nobody else is watching. When nobody else is telling you to do it, you're pushing yourself to do it."

-- **Aaron Donald,** defensive tackle for the Los Angeles Rams of the NFL. He was an All-American at Pittsburgh and was selected by the Rams in the first round of the 2014 NFL Draft.

He's regarded as one of the greatest defensive players of all time and received a record three Defensive Player of the Year Awards, Pro Bowl selections in all eight of his seasons, and seven first-team All-Pro honors.

Déjà vu. "I'll be running, the ball will be in the air, and I'll feel like I've been in that moment before. It's basically Deja vu, like an active Deja vu, I guess you could say.

-- **Davante Adams**, On March 18, 2022, the Packers traded Adams to the Las Vegas Raiders in exchange for their 2022 first-round pick and a second-round pick.

Along with the trade, Adams signed a five-year, $141.25M deal, making him the highest-paid wide receiver in the NFL at the time of the signing.

The trade also reunited Adams with his college quarterback Derek Carr, with both playing together at Fresno State from 2012 to 2013. [49]

Dedicated. "If my mother put on a helmet and shoulder pads and a uniform that wasn't the same as the one I was wearing, I'd run over her if she was in my way. And I love my mother."

For a Football Fan Who Has Everything by Bruce Miller & Team Golfwell

-- Bo Jackson.

What was the coldest NFL game (so far)? It is difficult to say depending on temperature and windchill index. Most say it was the famous "Ice Bowl" at Lambeau Field in Green Bay. This game is also considered to be one of the greatest NFL Championship games ever.

The "Ice Bowl" took place in 1967 between the Cowboys and the Packers in Green Bay. According to NFL Communications, the game-time temperature was 13 degrees below zero at the start of the game and went down to minus -18 F at the end of the game when Bart Starr squeezed it in from short yardage to win the game.

Even though the wind chill factor was around - 45 to -50 F, it was surprisingly attended by 50,861 screaming fans -- a sellout crowd.

Moving the ball wasn't easy. A layer of condensation formed between the tarp and the field and when the tarp was removed, it instantly froze. Both teams were playing on frozen tundra like the lands above the Artic Circle. The Packers won 21-17 and both teams had total yardages below 200 yards (Packers 195, Dallas 192). Still, you must admire Green Bay and Dallas fans who attended this sell-out Championship game. [50]

Survival. "Pro football is like nuclear warfare. There are no winners, only survivors."

-- **Frank Gifford.** Player, actor, and television sports commentator. After a 12-year playing career as a halfback and flanker for the New York Giants of the National Football League (NFL), he was a play-by-play announcer and commentator for 27 years on ABC's Monday Night Football

I didn't mean it! Darius Reynaud, playing for the Tennessee Titans, on the opening kickoff of the 2013 season fielded the kickoff with one foot out of the end zone and then immediately returned into the end zone and dropped a knee scoring the fastest points in NFL history (resulting in a 2-point safety for the opposing team, the Steelers). [51]

Reynaud caught the opening kickoff in the end zone, momentarily entered the field of play, and hesitatingly re-entered the end-zone as he apparently thought a touchback would be the best return option.

The officials originally ruled it as a touchback but opposing coach Mike Tomlin challenged since the ball was taken out of the end zone and then re-entered the end zone.

The ruling was overturned, and the Steelers were given a 2-point safety. [52]

"Watch where you throw the flag Ref!" On December 19, 1999, Cleveland played the Jacksonville Jaguars and **Orlando Brown** (an offensive tackle 6' 7" 360 lbs.) was hit in the right eye by a penalty flag weighted with ball bearings thrown by referee Jeff Triplette who apologized to him immediately. [53]

Orlando left the game but returned to the field shortly to shove Triplette, knocking him to the ground. Brown was ejected from the game and had to be escorted off the field by his teammates. Brown suffered temporary blindness and missed three seasons.

According to reports, he settled for a sum between $15 million and $25 million in 2002.

Alpha. The beginning. "We interrupt this marriage and bring you the football season."

Omega. The end. "Well, the football season is over. Now I'm going to get back to wishing it were football season again."

    -- Anon.

"Leadership is a matter of having people look at you and gain confidence. If you're in control, they're in control."

-- **Tom Landry**

Dream big. "If your dream ain't bigger than you, there's a problem with your dream."

-- **Deion Sanders,** "Neon Deion" NFL Hall of Famer and 14 seasons in the NFL. He also played outfielder with the New York Yankees, Atlanta Braves, Cincinnati Reds, and San Francisco Giants. He won two Super Bowl titles and made one World Series appearance in 1992. He is the only athlete to play in both a Super Bowl and a World Series. [54]

At the start of his career, one of the first things he did was to buy a beautiful home for his mother in Southwest Florida.

Just want to be here. "But at the end of the day, we all want to be here as a player. That's the goal, and that's why I work so dang hard."

-- **J. J. Watt**, Defensive end for the Arizona Cardinals

For a Football Fan Who Has Everything by Bruce Miller & Team Golfwell

We hope you enjoyed our book!

If you liked our book, we would sincerely appreciate your taking a few moments to leave a brief review.

Thank you again very much!

Team Golfwell and Bruce Miller

Bruce@TeamGolfwell.com

About the authors

Bruce Miller. A lawyer, businessman, world traveler, golf and football enthusiast, Golf Rules Official, actor, and author of over 40 books, a few being Amazon bestsellers, spends his days writing, studying, and constantly learning of the astounding, unexpected, and amazing events happening in the world today while exploring the brighter side of life.

He is a member of Team Golfwell, Authors, and Publishers.

Team Golfwell are bestselling authors and founders of the very popular 280,000+ member Facebook Group "Golf Jokes and Stories."

Their books have sold thousands of copies including several #1 bestsellers in Golf Coaching, Sports humor, and other categories.

We Want to Hear from You!

"There usually is a way to do things better and there is opportunity when you find it." - Thomas Edison

We love to hear your thoughts and suggestions on anything and please feel free to contact us at Bruce@TeamGolfwell.com

Other Books by Bruce Miller and Team Golfwell

For the Golfer Who Has Everything: A Funny Golf Book

For the Mother Who Has Everything: A Funny Book for Mother

For the Father Who Has Everything: A Funny Book for Father

For the Grandmother Who Has Everything: A Funny Book for Grandmothers

For the Grandfather Who Has Everything: A Funny Book for Grandfathers

The Funniest Quotations to Brighten Every Day: Brilliant, Inspiring, and Hilarious Thoughts from Great Minds

Jokes for Very Funny Kids (Ages 3 to 7): Funny Jokes, Riddles and More

Jokes for Very Funny Kids (Big & Little): Funny Jokes and Riddles Ages 9 - 12 and up and many more. 55

Brilliant Screen-Free Stuff to Do with Kids: A Handy Reference for Parents & Grandparents!

And many more…

For a Football Fan Who Has Everything by Bruce Miller & Team Golfwell

Index

The Jaguars haven't been to a Super Bowl 1

It's the same thing 1

Two Detroit Lions fans died 2

Food 2

Training 3

God loves the Jets 3

Let them tell you 4

Basketball vs. Football. 4

No one noticed me 5

Immediate concern 7

I love my mother but… 9

Astroturf vs. grass 10

Has any game ever ended with a score of 2-0? 12

Easy game! 12

You probably already know this. 13

Watching football games. 15

Longest postseason drought 16

For a Football Fan Who Has Everything by Bruce Miller & Team Golfwell

Not shy 16

Hits 16

Dad Jokes 17

Headlines: NFL Cuts One Team 18

Tom Brady's will to win 18

Longest winning streak in football 19

No! Not Detroit! 21

Amelioration 22

Chasing 22

Baseball vs. Football 24

Undefeated teams in the regular season 24

Two opinions from Ike 25

Of course! 26

And have you ever wondered 27

Get the guillotine 27

Four Football Fans. 27

Qualifications for a lineman. 29

Say again? 32

Highest scoring game (so far). 32

For a Football Fan Who Has Everything by Bruce Miller & Team Golfwell

Trash talk joke.	32
Earned the right	33
Just joking!	33
The Winningest.	34
Vision gets the dreams started	35
Did you know?	35
Losing streaks.	35
Who's the leader of the band that's made for you and me.	36
Why I like football	37
I'm too sexy	37
Joshy Boucher?	38
Overcome	38
Dear Diary,	39
Busy night	42
Reflection	43
Super Bowl locations	43
Oh? You don't believe in me?	43
I'll show you	44
Life's experiences	44

Fire 46

Madden's humility 46

Narrowing it down 46

Reflection 47

Lucky beard 47

Champion 47

Why won't Lucy let Charlie Brown kick the football? ... 48

Turn it around 49

Life is like football 50

Prove something? 50

No coincidence 50

Exposing buttocks 51

Meaning 51

Good morning! 51

Class 52

Long medical history. 52

A silent tribute 52

Did you know this? 53

The passing of an NFL great 54

For a Football Fan Who Has Everything by Bruce Miller & Team Golfwell

Most points scored 55

The longest...game time.. 55

An old one 56

Dad joke 56

Say what? 57

It's truly the people 57

Ironhead 58

Unknown brother 58

He was fierce 59

Largest attended game (so far) 60

Determination 60

Free 60

Bart Starr's father 60

Dealing with it. 61

"Success isn't owned 62

On failures and wins – Coach Bum Phillips 63

What it is 64

Charger defense... 64

How I started 65

Contacting Tech Support	65
What work really is	67
What do rich people buy, Jimmy?	68
Practice	69
No promises	69
Tough Exam	69
This is how you play	70
Keep on keeping on	70
"The thing about football	71
Wives	71
The Oldest Rivalry	71
Getting ahead	72
Go for it	72
The enemy of the best	73
"I do that too with my assistant."	73
Two things	73
Stand by me	73
Intriguing questions.	74
They're just grown up now	74

For a Football Fan Who Has Everything by Bruce Miller & Team Golfwell

Could be anyone **75**

Talk to the best **75**

College team banter. **75**

Meaning of luck **78**

Dad joke **78**

An old one **78**

Father of American Football **78**

Good idea **80**

Sharks **81**

Stones **81**

Blindsided **81**

Only Bradshaw could say this **82**

Brett Favre's first-ever NFL completion **82**

Turn the TV on and get a beer **83**

Necessities -- When you gotta go. **84**

The shape of a football **84**

Pro teams' banter. **85**

Jim Brown. **86**

Second place isn't bad **87**

Team effort.	88
Would you rather?	88
Intimidation by osmosis	89
Who does Tom Brady look up to?	89
An old one	89
More pro banter.	90
100%	91
Mental toughness	91
No way.	92
Rugby	92
Comparison.	92
NFL record for most touchdowns	92
Turn me down?	93
Peyton Manning goes to heaven	93
No, not another one of those meetings!	94
First Afro-American.	94
What's really important	95
Legendary team	96
Don't give up	97

For a Football Fan Who Has Everything by Bruce Miller & Team Golfwell

Are NFL players big? 97

Female referees 97

Winter sports 98

Lack of talent doesn't matter 98

Grilled cheese 98

Emergency! 99

Giant Riddle 100

Largest and smallest NFL Stadiums 100

It's halftime in America 101

The Sunday checklist 102

Largest American Football Stadium 102

"We're going to score!" 104

Winning the Super Bowl 105

No necks 105

Thinking positive 105

It's no accident 106

Vince Lombardi 106

"It's not that hard to be good 109

Déjà vu 110

For a Football Fan Who Has Everything by Bruce Miller & Team Golfwell

Dedicated. 110

What was the coldest NFL game (so far 111

Survival. 112

I didn't mean it! 112

"Watch where you throw the flag Ref!" 113

Alpha. The beginning. 113

Omega. The end. 113

"Leadership 113

Just want to be here. 114

We hope you enjoyed our book! 115

About the authors 116

We Want to Hear from You! 117

Other Books by Bruce Miller and Team Golfwell 118

References

[1] Josh Allen, Wikipedia, Josh Allen, Wikipedia, https://en.wikipedia.org/wiki/Josh_Allen_(quarterback
[2] Ibid.
[3] Josh Allen, Wikipedia (quarterback), https://en.wikipedia.org/wiki/Josh_Allen_(quarterback)
[4] Wikipedia, Peyton Manning, https://en.wikipedia.org/wiki/Peyton_Manning
[5] Joe Namath, Wikipedia, https://en.wikipedia.org/wiki/Joe_Namath#Personal_life
[6] WegENT Network, https://wegrynenterprises.com/2022/03/24/report-1-in-4-americans-watch-5-hours-of-sports-weekly/
[7] Jack Tatum, Wikipedia, https://en.wikipedia.org/wiki/Jack_Tatum
[8] Canton Bulldogs, Wikipedia, https://en.wikipedia.org/wiki/Canton_Bulldogs
[9] Britannica.com, https://www.britannica.com/biography/Jim-Thorpe-American-athlete
[10] Sports.jrank.org, https://sports.jrank.org/pages/4844/Thorpe-Jim-Related-Biography-Coach-Glenn-Scobey-Pop-Warner.html
[11] Dwight D Eisenhower, Wikipedia, https://en.wikipedia.org/wiki/Dwight_D._Eisenhower
[12] Ravens-Steelers Rivalry, Wikipedia, https://en.wikipedia.org/wiki/Ravens%E2%80%93Steelers_rivalry
[13] University of Notre Dame Archives, http://archives.nd.edu/research/texts/rocknespeech2.htm
[14] Highest scoring NFL games, Wikipedia, https://en.wikipedia.org/wiki/List_of_highest-scoring_NFL_games

[15] Tom Brady, Wikipedia, https://en.wikipedia.org/wiki/Tom_Brady
[16] Wikipedia, List of National Football League career rushing yards leader, https://en.wikipedia.org/wiki/List_of_National_Football_League_career_rushing_yards_leaders
[17] List of longest NFL losing streaks, Wikipedia, https://en.wikipedia.org/wiki/List_of_National_Football_League_longest_losing_streaks
[18] Ibid.
[19] Davante Adams, Wikipedia, https://en.wikipedia.org/wiki/Davante_Adams
[20] Patrick Mahones, Wikipedia, https://en.wikipedia.org/wiki/Patrick_Mahomes
[21] John Madden, Wikipedia, https://en.wikipedia.org/wiki/John_Madden
[22] George Blanda, Wikipedia, https://en.wikipedia.org/wiki/George_Blanda
[23] Adam Vinatieri, Wikipedia, https://en.wikipedia.org/wiki/Adam_Vinatieri
[24] Yahoo sports. https://sports.yahoo.com/longest-shortest-games-nfl-history-023910108.html#:~:text=Garo%20Yepremian%
[25] Craig Heyward, Wikipedia, https://en.wikipedia.org/wiki/Craig_Heyward
[26] NBC Sports, https://www.nbcsports.com/video/joe-theismann-discusses-changing-pronunciation-last-name
[27] Ibid.
[28] Southern Maryland Chronicle, https://southernmarylandchronicle.com/2021/10/15/nfls-biggest-attendances-to-date
[29] Don Shula, Wikipedia, https://en.wikipedia.org/wiki/Don_Shula#Later_life_and_death

[30] Marca.com, "NFL History: What is the oldest rivalry in NFL History?" https://www.marca.com/en/nfl/2022/01/12/61df369f22601d92268b4606.html
[31] History of American football, Wikipedia, Wikipedia, American Football, https://en.wikipedia.org/wiki/History_of_American_football
[32] Ibid.
[33] Sportscasting.com, https://www.sportscasting.com/terry-bradshaw-checked-hospital-using-tom-bradys-name-brady-5-years-old/
[34] CBS Sports, https://www.cbssports.com/nfl/news/remember-when-brett-favre-completes-1st-nfl-pass-to-himself/
[35] Ibid.
[36] Sportscasting, https://www.sportscasting.com/nfl-how-do-football-players-go-to-the-bathroom-during-a-game/
[37] Ibid.
[38] Jim Brown, Wikipedia, https://en.wikipedia.org/wiki/Jim_Brown
[39] Ibid.
[40] Charles Follis, Wikipedia, https://en.wikipedia.org/wiki/Charles_Follis
[41] Horrigan, Joe. "Early Black Professionals" (PDF). Coffin Corner. Professional Football Researchers Association. Archived from the original (PDF) on November 27, 2010. Retrieved April 18, 2013.
[42] Sportscasting, https://www.sportscasting.com/the-hottest-nfl-games-in-history-roasted-these-legendary-quarterbacks/
[43] Ibid.
[44] Illinois Sports Facility Authority, https://www.isfauthority.com/facilities/soldier-field
[45] Michigan Stadium, Wikipedia, https://en.wikipedia.org/wiki/Michigan_Stadium

[46] Narendra_Modi_Stadium, Wikipedia, https://en.wikipedia.org/wiki/Narendra_Modi_Stadium
[47] Wikipedia, Vince Lombardi, https://en.wikipedia.org/wiki/Vince_Lombardi
[48] Ibid.
[49] Davante Adams, Wikipedia, https://en.wikipedia.org/wiki/Davante_Adams
[50] 1967 NFL Championship Game, Wikipedia, https://en.wikipedia.org/wiki/1967_NFL_Championship_Game
[51] Darius Reynaud, Wikipedia, https://en.wikipedia.org/wiki/Darius_Reynaud
[52] Ibid.
[53] Orlando Brown, Wikipedia, https://en.wikipedia.org/wiki/Orlando_Brown_(American_football)
[54] Deion Sanders, Wikipedia, https://en.wikipedia.org/wiki/Deion_Sanders#Professional_football_career
[55] Ibid.

www.ingramcontent.com/pod-product-compliance
Lightning Source LLC
LaVergne TN
LVHW092314300325
807293LV00001B/4